# DON'T TIE YOURSELF UP IN "NOTS"

D1057089

ISBN: 0-9629230-0-1

PRINTED IN THE UNITED STATES OF AMERICA

# DON'T TIE YOURSELF UP IN "NOTS"

HOW TO UNTIE YOURSELF FROM
THE CAN "NOTS" AND SHOULD "NOTS"
OF LIFE.

By:

David P. Schloss

to my parents,
Bill & Jan Schloss
with love and admiration.
Thank you for being my biggest fans
as well as my best friends.

# ABOUT THE AUTHOR

Dave Schloss has given many financial and positive thinking seminars to the general public to not only introduce to them how to develop a gameplan for financial success, but also to instill in them the attitude that they can achieve this success themselves.

Dave has spent most of the last fifteen years involved in real estate education, as well as the areas of sales and investments. During this period he has sold and/or invested in everything from condominiums to large commercial office buildings, and has helped others invest thousands of dollars in both real estate and securities.

Dave is currently licensed in real estate, insurance, syndications, securities, mortgages, and real estate education.

# WHY ANOTHER BOOK ON THE SUBJECT

# OF POSITIVE MENTAL ATTITUDE?

It is not just a book about positive mental attitude. It's a book, that covers all phases of being a success. They are, winning financially and physically, as well as winning mentally.

This book is designed to be fast paced and easy to read, to get directly to the point, because I wanted something that people could read and apply immediately. We have all read books that are long and drawn out, and have taken forever to get to the point. For most of us, if it takes a long time to read and/or understand the contents of a book, we are less likely to apply it to our lives.

For all the schooling that we went through, no one ever taught us the power of one of the most important ingredients we could ever learn in our life, the power of positive thinking. You can get good grades, be very smart, do all the right things and be in all the right places, but with the wrong frame of mind still not succeed at life.

People succeed in life more often because of attitude, than aptitude. The world is full of people with talent and skill that have not succeeded. It's also full of people with much less ability who have succeeded in much bigger ways. The difference? More often than not, a positive winning attitude!

Why another book on positive mental attitude? Because the army of negativism is recruiting people daily, and I don't want you to enlist. But above all, I believe that any one of us can untie the "nots" that bind our lives if someone will just show us how!

# TABLE OF CONTENTS

# CHAPTER ONE

# A SEVENTH GRADE LESSON
# FOR A LIFETIME

We probably all learned the "Golden Rule" when we were very young. "Do unto others, as you would have them do unto you."

These eleven words say more about how to conduct relationships, both business and personal than any ever written.

It doesn't matter whether you're the leader of a big or small business, have many friends or only a few. It comes down to treating people properly, having respect for them, and finding their best qualities.

Respect is a two way street. It is like trust, it can't be purchased for any price, it can only be earned.

Respect as a leader comes from never asking someone to do something that you haven't done, or wouldn't do yourself. It comes from being consistent. It comes from standing firm in your beliefs. People won't follow or believe in anyone who keeps changing his mind on the issues.

I believe the good leaders have mastered the art of

praise as a reward and motivator. If the praise is sincere and warranted, give it. Do it in public whenever possible. But what about the times when someone is headed in the wrong direction? If you must criticize, do it in private. A rule we must try to live by if we must criticize is, two pats on the back for each kick in the rear. Meaning, start out with a positive, end with a positive, and sandwich the criticism in between.

My first experience with the power of praise was in the seventh grade. It was a science class. To me, nothing was worse. To put things in perspective, you should know that achieving A's and B's during my first twelve years in school was rare for me. In fact, I didn't start making good grades until I entered college. Coincidentally, that was when school started costing me money.

But, back to the seventh grade. There is not much doubt I didn't like school very much, and had even less concern for science class. It was the first day of the new school year, and the first year we had different classrooms for each class. I remember entering science class as if it were yesterday. There were about 35 chairs in the room; however, 10 of them were on one side by themselves. No one sat in those 10 chairs. We all thought something was wrong with them. So we filled the room in the remaining 25 seats. That is when the teacher came in and explained that those chairs were going to be for his "A" students only. I thought this was amusing, but paid little attention.

As the weeks went by, four or five students earned "A" averages, and with it, the right to sit in one of those chairs.

This still didn't interest me until one day another teacher came in and asked our instructor about "those chairs." "Those are my "A" students, the real brains," he replied. The visitor said, "Oh, I see." Then without saying a word, he cast a glance at the rest of us. His look said it all.

Right then I knew that for me, just being average, a part of the crowd, was not good enough. I wanted to sit in one of those chairs so badly I could taste it. It hadn't yet dawned on me that to do so would mean I would have to carry an "A" average in science class. I had never carried an "A" average in anything before, but I didn't care, because all I could think about was sitting in one of those seats. I suddenly hated the thought of being grouped with the average people. I wanted to be somebody. Over the next semester I worked harder at science class than I have ever worked at anything before, and I made it. I got my chair!

I learned two very important lessons from that science teacher. One, he motivated by praising the "A" students and not by downgrading the rest of the class. Two, I learned, for what was the first time, what it was like to focus on a goal and go for it.

The analogy is that many leaders and managers today don't praise their people enough. In fact, many don't praise them at all. When you are at work and doing things right, nobody notices. Only when you do something wrong, do you hear anything. Most managers today could learn a valuable lesson from my seventh grade science teacher.

Most everyone underestimates both the power of praise and the harm of criticism. Strong praise as well as damaging criticism can stay with you for weeks, months, or even years.

Think about how you felt the last time someone sincerely praised your efforts. Who doesn't want to hear what a great job they are doing, or how nice they look, or how valuable they are to their organization? How did it affect your actions the rest of the day? Did you stand a little taller, walk a little faster, do a little better job? Do you want to feel that way again? Of course you do, who doesn't? Do you have to wait to be praised? No, because one of the great things about praise is that both parties win! Not only the person who receives it, but also the person who gives it.

So if you want to recreate that uplifting feeling in

yourself, go out and give someone sincere praise and see if it doesn't do as much for you as it does for them. The more you give, the more you receive. I also believe this goes for criticism as well. So give what you want in return!

The bottom line is, if you're a leader in your organization, or even if you're not, whether we are talking about your business or personal life, be positive! Motivate with positives, be consistent, and earn the respect and trust of others through your actions.

Develop a sincere interest in people, and work on becoming a good listener. To be a good listener, you must really hear what people are saying, don't just listen. Tune in, don't be guilty of selective deafness, which is hearing only what you want to hear. Look them in the eye and don't interrupt.

Acquire the ability to empathize with people. Having the ability to put yourself in their shoes, along with being a good listener are the building blocks of good relationships.

Zig Ziglar has always been one of my favorite motivational speakers, and in his book <u>TOP</u> <u>PERFOR-MANCE</u> he shares with us two important insights with regard to treating people properly. First, "People don't care how much you know, until they know how much you care...about them!" Second, "You can have everything in life you want, if you will just help enough other people get what they want!"

What's the bottom line? Show people you care about them and you will both come out winners!

# CHAPTER TWO

# GETTING STARTED..... AND WHY MOST PEOPLE DON'T

Overcoming procrastination is something that can't wait until tomorrow. Procrastination is one of the biggest roadblocks that prevent people from attaining what they want from life. The people that say they will someday do this, or that, never will.

The reasons? The path of least resistance, lack of direction, fear, lack of knowledge, etc. all of which we will discuss in the upcoming pages.

But first, let's take a look at life, the ultimate game. There is an analogy that can be drawn between life and games, and that is both have a time limit, and both have goals. The major difference is, in life, we are all players. We are in the game whether we want to be or not and it is up to us to determine to what degree we are going to play.

Our clock in life started running the day we were born, however we don't know when it's going to stop. Therefore to be successful, we must start now. But how do you start now? How do you kindle a fire to drive you to new successes? That depends on you.

As you read what follows here, one of the things that will help you most, is an open mind. Many people say that being open minded is a way of life for them. However the first time something new is suggested, they snap back with, "That will never work." Or some say, " O.K., I'll try your crazy idea, but if it doesn't work, we're going back to the old way." These are not examples of open mindedness. With those attitudes, what do you think the chances are for success?

You must be ready to accept new ideas, at least at face value. Take that which applies, absorb it, and validate it from a third party source. You must discard your ready- made answers and solutions that you now have in order to have the opportunity to find new directions.

Everybody has something they have always wanted to do, something they really believe in. That belief is the first step to getting out of their easy chair.

Getting motivated is all a mindset. It is attitude. For example, you are on the couch watching T.V. and you remember the yard needs cutting, but you are too tired. Suddenly, the phone rings and it's a friend who wants to play tennis. Just as suddenly, you're ready to play. Because cutting the grass is not something you wanted to do, you mentally told yourself you were too tired. But were you?

In fact, most of us can probably think of things we might not be eager to do. Waxing the car, cleaning out the garage, or fixing something around the house would all certainly be on this list. However, playing basketball or going to a football game might sound good. It is not laziness, it's attitude.

It takes more energy to play basketball than clean out the garage, but some of us would still rather play basketball. So we don't consider ourselves lazy, just particular about how we spend our time. We usually find the time to do the things we really want to do. The things we are really excited about.

This thought process is applied to your business time, as well as your leisure time. Take a moment to think about your job. If your experience is anything like mine, quitting time at work usually means a stampede for the door. Those who stay, usually do so because they feel like they should, not because they want to.

Let's hold up the stampede for a moment, and imagine that your boss met everyone at the door and said, "I would like everybody to work extra hours today, without pay until I feel like we should stop." Would everyone look at him as if he had three eyes?

However, have you ever been engrossed in

something and lost all track of time? Did you wind up working many hours on whatever it was without regard to pay? Sure, all of us have. The difference is we were doing what we were excited about, not what the boss thought we should be excited about.

In life, the reason that most people never really get started is because they fail to find anything worthwhile to get fired up about. If you look back through history, you'll see a common denominator among many great people, and that is, they found a cause to champion. They had a burning desire, a passion.

It's the passion to succeed that drives many to the top of their profession, whether it is in a corporate structure or as head of their own company. It's passion that many athletes have about their sport that compels them to greatness after injuries would have inhibited others from even playing.

If you can get on fire for something that you feel strongly about, or love to do, your vehicle is already in gear. It is imperative that you find your passion, your desire in life.

Taking this a step further, for your life to improve, *you* must improve. Think of your car. If it doesn't take you where you want to go, what would you do? You would probably fix it, or replace it, right? It's the same with your actions and beliefs. If they haven't achieved what you want in life, maybe you should fix or change them. If you're not happy with where you've been, and you don't make changes to improve yourself, it's a cinch you won't be happy with where you're going.

Take the average job in corporate America today. It's been said that most people are paid just enough so they won't quit, and work just hard enough so they won't get fired. It is a known fact that a big percentage of Americans today do not like or enjoy what they do for a living. So why don't they change? When you ask them they answer, "What else can I do?" or "It's too late now for me to change." These people have lost their ability to dream and it's obvious. They act like it is a sentence they must carry out. It's as if the judge in life's court of attitudes has sentenced them to a life of mediocrity. They believe they no longer have a choice, that this is the way it must be.

There is another group who have lost their ability to dream, but they are more difficult to recognize. These are the people who say they have big dreams, but if you asked them what they would do if you handed them $100,000, they don't have a clue, and their response is something like, "Oh, that's crazy." What's crazy, is not having the attitude that you will someday have to deal with what you will do with $100,000.

17

The first group, when it comes to dreams, doesn't say it or believe it. The second group says it, but doesn't believe it. Both are heading for the same location, just taking different routes.

Most of these people weren't always that way. How about you? Think back to when you were a kid. It is natural for kids to dream, and the sky is the limit. I remember myself and all the other kids dreaming about being major league baseball players, or jet pilots, or rock stars. We thought we could do anything. I don't remember any of us, or for that matter, any kid I ever met, when asked what he wanted to do when he grew up, answer with a list of things he couldn't do. It was always positive. I'm going to be this, or I'm going to be that.

But how often have we heard an adult say to a teenager, "Get those ridiculous ideas about being a professional athlete, or singer, or whatever, out of your head. You need to settle down and establish yourself." This is an example of the dream erosion factor at work.

People who had already lost their ability to dream told us that we needed to get the crazy ideas out of our heads and think about getting a good job. If you are constantly told by friends and relatives that your dreams are crazy, sooner or later you are likely to believe it, and when you do you are heading toward a life of being average and just getting by. Thank God the Thomas Edisons, Ben Franklins, and many others didn't stop dreaming.

Remember, it's never too late to begin dreaming and believing, because it's not where you have been, but where you are going that counts. But you must get started now! *Now* is the key word. The "I'll do it later" attitude is procrastination, and the talk of losers! Many say they are too old to start now and that life has passed them by. Again, it's not a matter of age, it's a matter of attitude! Do you know people, retired or not, who just sit around waiting to pass away? Have you ever thought that these people could be having fun and doing so much more with their life? Do you feel sorry for them? Do you promise yourself it won't happen to you? Do you think they said the same thing when they were younger?

I don't know about you, but when I see an older person who is active and living life, I find it exhilarating because it shows me the way things can be, not the way that some think it must be.

Learn to dream again and get fired up about life, find something to feel strongly about and be willing to pay...

# CHAPTER THREE

# THE PRICE OF SUCCESS

Success is a personal thing. It's not what others think, it's what you think. Have you honestly accomplished what you wanted to in life? Have you done all that you set out to do? Have you come close? The key words are "honestly accomplished." You can lie to yourself, but you can't fool yourself.

The reason most people are not happy with the answers to the above questions is because they were never willing to pay the price.

The two variables that must be considered are desire and time. Some people have desire, but when they don't see big results quickly they say, "It doesn't work for me." Some plod along for years without ever making any real effort and say, "I've been working at it for years... nothing terrific has ever happened to me. I guess this is what I have to look forward to the rest of my life."

This person is right, and wrong. He has not been working at it, just working. With his current attitude, he is right when he says this is what he has to look forward to, because he has planted the seeds of mediocrity.

The reason so few ever achieve what they want in life is because so few ever combine real effort (desire) for as long as it takes to win (time).

That is paying the price! You must be willing to make a real effort toward your goals for whatever time it takes to succeed. That is not saying give it a good year or two; rather whatever time it takes. If your goals are solid and your road map is right, then go for it!

Most can't do that. They don't expect it to really work, so it doesn't. Realize that success can be learned. That if you pay the price, success can be yours. People aren't born successful. It comes from trying over and over again.

Take even the simplest of things, such as tying your shoes. You are fairly successful at it now, but did you start out that way or did it take you several times to get the hang of it? What about walking? Did you do that right away or did you gradually accomplish it after first learning to crawl?

Did it ever cross your mind that learning to walk was too much trouble, and maybe it would be better to just crawl around the rest of your life? No? Why not? Maybe it was because you had very few negative seeds in your mind at that time. Maybe it was also because everyone else was walking, and encouraging you to do the same. The point is that you kept at it until you succeeded, even though it was tough, and you got a few bumps and bruises along the way.

Being a success at life is a much tougher goal, and there are some obvious differences between this goal and the goal of walking. First, we all have some negatives that we have picked up along the way that we must constantly fight. Second, there are very few people applauding each step that we take, and constantly encouraging us as they did in our goal to walk. Regardless of whether we are talking about learning to walk or succeeding at life, you must keep at it, pay the price, and overcome the bumps and bruises until you succeed.

Most people don't understand why they are not "at the top" immediately, or soon thereafter. It's because it just doesn't work that way. If it did, we would all be "at the top."

The reason the "top" is great, is because it is *not* achieved by everyone. For us to achieve success, we must stay focused on our goals for whatever time it takes for us to win.

Most everyone wants to be successful, but few are willing to pay the price. This goes back to an earlier stated theory regarding the path of least resistance. If the will to be mediocre is stronger than the will to succeed, you are programming your future to give you a view of the past that you probably won't like.

Paying the price is picking yourself up, time and time again, until you succeed. Some will do this for awhile, some a while longer, but few long enough to succeed. Most people work at something until it is just about to pay off, then they quit. They get so close to seeing the light at the end of the tunnel, but give up, not realizing just how near they were to success. Remember, water does nothing at 210 or 211 degrees, but that extra degree or two makes all the difference.

Nationally known sales trainer, Tom Hopkins said, "I am not judged by the number of times I fail but by the number of times I succeed, and the number of times I succeed is in direct proportion to the number of times I can fail, and keep on trying."

Develop the mindset of never giving up. Remember, failing is not bad, quitting is. You never fail until you quit.

Understand the world is not perfect, and since no human is either, temporary setbacks are inevitable. Everyone makes mistakes. The difference is, successful people view mistakes only as a learning experience and not as failure. This experience is just another way something cannot be accomplished, it's not the end. Therefore, we can't be afraid to make mistakes, and we must realize that since they are a part of life, they shouldn't stop us, only show us what needs to be corrected so that we can succeed next time.

The winners in life keep trying long after the losers have given up. That is what paying the price is all about.

# CHAPTER FOUR

# LEARNING THE RULES

People can't lead you where they haven't been. Find someone who has made it in the area in which you want to make it, and do what they do. These thoughts went through my mind as I sat in college classes being taught finance and investments.

Looking back now, I found that I was right. Most of the investments we were advised were best, were the same ones that are responsible for a large number of Americans retiring today on income that is at the poverty level.

Most of the time, the instructors that were teaching the courses had never accomplished any financial independence for themselves. It is not surprising that most of the students never did either. The teachers had book knowledge, and I'm sure you will agree, classroom situations and real life are usually very different. There is nothing wrong with having book knowledge, but it is no substitute for experience. Unfortunately, finding those who really have the experience can take work.

I decided in my early twenties that I wanted to own a home. The only problem was, I couldn't afford it. As far as potential home ownership problems go, I would classify this as one of the biggest. Obviously, talking to my friends in the rental community was going to be a waste of time. Talking to most of my friends who owned a home didn't help much either, because most had a second income from a spouse and saved 20% of the down payment to get into the home. Not having much money or spousal income, things looked bleak. I was saving all that I could, but the house prices kept going up.

One day I was talking to a friend who suggested that I buy a house "nothing down." This of course is the technique of buying a home without the necessity of a down payment. I asked him how to do this, and he responded that, he didn't know, but had heard it was possible.

I had recently obtained my real estate license, and didn't remember anything about buying real estate without any money down being mentioned in the course. I set about asking everyone connected with the real estate business how I could learn about this and the answers ranged from, "I don't know," to "It's impossible," to "Only the rich can do it," and so on.

Now, of course, if you stay up late and turn on

your cable T.V., you will see many people telling you how to buy real estate without cash by way of buying their tapes.

One day I ran across someone who said he was in a club that consisted of individuals buying property with little or no money down. He invited me to come along. He didn't know it but I was going anyway, invitation or not.

As soon as I arrived I began to seek out those who had done it from those who were just there to watch.

Within the next few months I bought my first home. It was brand new, from the developer, and cost me a total of $855.00 out of my pocket to close. If I had listened to my friends, I would have needed thousands. If I had tried to save the money toward a down payment, I would probably still be saving today.

The moral is, success leaves evidence. Whatever it is you want from life, you have to find people who are already successfully doing it, and copy them. Do what they do, think like they think. It stands to reason that if they are successful, and you do exactly what they did, you should have a very good chance of being successful too. There is no need to re-invent the wheel. Why do it differently if there is already a system in place that works?

It's better to hang around with those who have made a million and lost it, than with those who have never made it at all. Most millionaires today will tell you that going broke doesn't scare them because they have the knowledge and experience to build their fortunes again. Those who have never made it don't have a clue, and in their minds, no hope.

Learn to seek out people who have "done it." This may take time, but it's still faster than learning the hard way. Many learn the hard way, only because they don't see the benefit of learning from others knowledge and experience.

Go to seminars, arrive early and stay late. Get to talk with the speaker. Have a list of questions prepared and **written down.** There is nothing worse than waiting a long time to talk to the lecturer, and then when your opportunity arrives, you only remember one question. While you are waiting, observe those asking knowledgeable questions and try to meet them as well as the speaker. Pay attention, be a good listener, and take good notes. Make your time count!

Remember, as important as it is to listen to the experts, it is just as important to ignore the non-experts. This could be tough, because the non-experts could include, (and probably do) your friends and relatives. Everyone will want to give you advice. Remember to look at your well-meaning advisor and ask yourself one important question: Has this person accomplished what I want in life? The answer will tell you whether or not to heed their advice.

# CHAPTER FIVE

# GETTING POSITIVE AND LEARNING TO STAY THAT WAY

Almost anybody can be positive for a while, but few can remain that way long enough to accomplish their goals in life. Why? There are two reasons for this. One, most people are negative and love to see you that way too. And two, most people wish instead of goal set. For instance, people say, "I wish I could win the lottery," or "I wish I was rich," or "I wish I was successful."

Goals are the road map to success, and without them, people are lost. Negativism creeps in and they hear their friends' words of failure. We will spend time with proper goal setting in a later chapter, but for now let's go back to reason one. Many people around us are negative.

Of the two reasons for not being able to maintain a positive attitude, this is by far the most detrimental. Most tend to take the path of least resistance, both mentally and physically. It is easier to lie around the house, than to do what is necessary to win at life. It is easier to think negative thoughts than positive ones.

Negativism is a disease and unfortunately it is contagious. It's all around us. The words, "I can't" or "That's impossible" were created by humans.

Let's look at some of the things we hear regularly that are negative. How about the news? There is not a whole lot of positive things reported on television. News used to be only 15 minutes in the evening in the 1960's. It is now one and a half to two hours every evening. Some are lucky enough to have cable T.V., where they have access to 24 hours of basically nega-tive news every day. It's important to stay current, however there are only so many bombings, stabbings, shootings, and bankruptcies that one person can handle. Even the weatherman has gotten into the act. It's not 70% chance of sun, it's 30% chance of rain. How about the sportscaster talking about sudden death instead of sudden victory? By the time the average child turns 18 years old, he or she has heard "no" many thousands of times. We are being conditioned to lose, conditioned to believe that we cannot be successful.

I am reminded of a story about the fleas in the jar. To my knowledge, fleas only know how to do two things, jump and bite. The story goes, that if you put some fleas in a jar and cover it with a lid, they will begin to jump. If it wasn't for the lid they could jump to freedom. Because the lid is there, every time they jump they hit their heads. This will go on for quite awhile until they are conditioned to jump just high enough so that they won't hit their heads on the lid of the jar. It is at this point that you could remove the lid and the fleas will stay in the jar, conditioned by their previous experiences. Even though freedom is possible, they believe it can't be achieved, therefore they will never attain it.

There is a strong parallel between the fleas and many people today. So many people are convinced that they can't succeed, because they have hit their heads on the lid of their jar of life for so long that they think winning at life is no longer possible. However, unlike the fleas, they placed the lid there themselves. Remember, the only limits you will have in your life are the ones *you* place there.

Most of us start out being praised for everything we do. Standing up was a big deal, our first step, walking, etc.. But then, as we grew up, we learned the words "can't" and "impossible." Many had a grand opening of the excuse factory. That is the part of your brain that produces excuses why you won't succeed.

We must stop making excuses and start looking for reasons why we will succeed. I met a person last week who was working as a clerk in a store. After we talked for a while, he began to tell me about his personal situation.  Bills, lousy job, having no money, etc.. I told him he could turn it around if he really wanted to. He said that he has always had problems like these and he always will.

With his current attitude, I would have to agree with him.  Art Williams, Founder of A.L. Williams, Inc. says, "Life will give you whatever you'll accept." This clerk has accepted these problems, so this is what he has to look forward to in the future. Anyone who wants to turn their life around strongly enough, can do it.

Life is meant to be a self-fulfilling prophesy. That is, it will turn out the way you see it turning out. A good example of this is the statement made by a head football coach part way through a recent NFL season. His team was expected to do fairly well that year, but after a mediocre start, he commented something close to the following. His team was playing so poorly, that they probably would not win another game the rest of the year.

He was trying to inspire his team with this comment, however the result was that they lost most of their remaining games and finished out of the playoffs.

Another example, closer to home, was a bumper sticker that read, "I may rise, but I refuse to shine." It was attached to a car that had an approximate market value of $250. The driver matched his car in physical appearance. He certainly lived up to his prediction. I believe your life will turn out pretty much the way that you expect it to turn out. Learn to develop positive vision, the ability to see great things for yourself, and you're half-way there.

As stated earlier, most people don't want to see you succeed. They may not necessarily want to see you fail, they just don't want you to win. It is easier for them that way. There are many stories relative to this concept and one of them has to do with a box of land crabs. If you leave the lid off, eventually one will try to crawl to freedom. What do you think the rest of the crabs do? They grab one of it's legs and pull it back in.

It's not all that different in life. We talked about having a dream and going for it. People will "pull you back in" by telling you that you can't do it. They will tell you they have known others who have tried it and failed and that you should forget it.

Perseverance is your ally. I believe, that it is your most important ally, and a very essential ingredient in the building of a winning attitude.

There is a story about a man that not only failed in business, his girlfriend passed away, he suffered a nervous breakdown, and lost bids for public office seven separate times. What is significant about this?

The significance lies in the fact that after all of these setbacks, this man still succeeded, and in a big way. He was elected President of the United States! This incredible biographical sketch is of Abraham Lincoln.

Do you believe he would have achieved the office of the Presidency following all of those setbacks, if he demonstrated the amount of perseverance exhibited by many people today? I guess that we all know the answer to that! He certainly showed great tenacity to keep on fighting through the failures, until he finally succeeded.

Exceptional things are accomplished by exceptional people, and what makes people this way is attitude. Anyone can be a great person, if they develop the greatness inside first. That's right, you choose whether or not you want a winning attitude! You're not born with one or without one. It has been said that success and failure are on the same road, success is just farther on. The level of your determination is an indicator of your belief in yourself. If you're the type of person who keeps trying after others have stopped, your actions show you really believe in yourself and your ability.

The fight to stay positive is a constant battle. You have to believe in yourself. Stop saying, "I can't" or "It's impossible." You must constantly account for all negative thoughts such as these, and turn them into positive ones immediately. It can be difficult to account for all of your negative thoughts because it's so easy for them to sneak in. You must be on guard constantly.

Here is a good example. At the start of a particular day, a couple little things go wrong that prompt you to say, "It's going to be one of those days." Well, you are setting the program for it. When you analyze it, these couple of bad things could have happened in the span of 15-20 minutes, and with this negative thinking, you are laying the ground work for the next 12-16 hours. Remember, turning around these little negative phrases may not be easy at first, but it's worth it. Be aware of it!

You have to be willing to be slightly controversial. After all, by being positive, you're going to be in the minority.

Most people can have a positive attitude once in a while. Usually, this is when the outside forces around them, such as people or events, are in a positive state. The tough part is being positive even when you don't feel positive. This means you can't wait for these surrounding factors to generate excitement for you, you must be able to generate your own enthusiasm from within.

As previously stated your attitude is everything.

It is the difference between winning and losing in life. To win, you must think successfully everyday, not just now and then.

Wouldn't it be nice to be able to buy a positive attitude on those days when you didn't have one? You could just go to the drug store and purchase a bottle of positive attitude pills. Of course, you wouldn't need a prescription and it would be impossible to overdose. The more you took, the longer you would stay positive. A bottle of these would make a great gift. Do you know of anyone who could use some of these pills?

This is a great fantasy, but unfortunately it doesn't work that way. If it did, everyone would have a bottle of positive attitude pills in their medicine cabinet. Getting positive and staying positive is your challenge and yours alone.

Excuses are the main reason that people don't stay positive. "My life is a wreck," "I don't have the time," "Good things don't happen to me," etc. If you work at convincing yourself that you can't do it, you will be a success, but it will be at failing. Excuses don't count for anything.

It has been said that you can choose your friends, but you can't choose your relatives. So choose your friends wisely. Associate with positive outgoing people who have direction in their lives. Learn to avoid people who are always putting themselves or others down.

Negative people are experts in how to wallow in self pity. They couldn't find a positive in something if it bit them. These people are negative because they no longer have dreams. They depress themselves. Even if things are going well they will find a negative to dwell upon. Pretty soon their shoulders droop, their heads drop, their voices slow and ... well, you know the rest. In other words, they are not born negative, they have to work at it.

Remember, it's not the action, it's your reaction that will determine your degree of success. When you make a decision to go after something, make sure you are on fire for it. Learn to get focused and commit to a goal.

Put up pictures or drawings throughout your home as constant reminders of your next objective. Whenever you start feeling negative, look at the pictures and tell yourself goals are not accomplished by negative people. When I have suggested to some people that they should display pictures of their dreams, some responded with, "It sounds a little silly," or "Someone will laugh." You realize of course, that the people who are going to be laughing are those too afraid to dream for themselves. Don't let what others say stop you. Your true strength comes from within.

You have to believe in your heart, without reservation, that you know what's best for you. You have to be "you," but you have to start today being the best "you," you can be.

This is the beginning of programming...

# CHAPTER SIX

# THE WORLD'S MOST
# INCREDIBLE COMPUTER

Have you ever stopped to think about the incredibility of the human brain? It has the ability to process thoughts and images at an unbelievable pace.

We call it a computer, but there are obviously many differences. Two of the most important ones are, unlike a computer, you can only control a portion of what gets programmed, and your brain has no erase button.

From the day you are born what you see and hear, both consciously and subconsciously, are programmed into your "computer." Your "computer," you realize is programmed mostly by others. Friends, relatives, T.V., radio, etc., all play a big part in the programming.

I remember when I was a kid, my parents accused me of knowing T.V. commercials better than my school work and they were right! I knew everything that went on a Big Mac and could sing along with any jingle. I was getting A's in commercial memorization and C's in school. One of the reasons was that T.V. did a better job of programming than my teachers.

Judging from what we see around us not much has changed today. Outside sources such as T.V., radio, friends, and relatives are still telling us how to act, what to wear, and what to buy. How do *you* spell relief? Is it, R -O- L- A -I -D -S ? Who are you "in good hands with?" What car is "engineered like no other car in the world?"

As I stated, most of what has been programmed into our "computer" has been put there by others. That would be fine if most of it helped us to be positive and successful and charged up about life. Unfortunately, most people today are not happy with what they do for a living and don't really have enough money to do the things they want to do; they are retiring on meager incomes and we are being programmed by them. Is there any hope for us? YES! Because unlike a real computer, we can think for ourselves and chart our own course.

Since we have the power to choose, why not get in the habit of choosing the right things for ourselves. We must begin programming our subconscious minds in a positive way immediately. Dr. Joseph Murphy, in his book, THE POWER OF YOUR SUBCONSCIOUS MIND tells us, "You are a gardener, and you are planting seeds (thoughts) in your subconscious mind all day long, based on your habitual thinking. As you sow in your subconscious mind, so shall you reap in your body and environment." He further states, "The main point to remember is once the subconscious mind accepts an idea, it begins to execute it." Your subconscious mind is always working, which is why you are what you believe. The first step, as stated earlier, is to begin positive programming now.

We have the power of imagination. This is incredibly powerful and can be one of your greatest allies. It can also be your greatest roadblock. Imagine, if you will, three diving boards. One is at five feet, another is at fifteen feet, and the third is at seventy-five feet.

What are you imagining as you stand out at the end of the five foot board? Making a big splash? Getting wet? Having fun? How about the fifteen foot board? A little nervous? Maybe, but imagining a successful entry into the water is not difficult. Now you are standing on the seventy- five foot board. What are you imagining? Some people are thinking about entry, and speed of entry. Some are just thinking about the pain of entry. Others are not even thinking about water, they are imagining being blown off course and hitting the concrete surrounding the pool area. Then there are a few just thinking about growing old and living out the rest of their days right up there on the board.

You have heard of your imagination running wild? You don't have to be on a high dive to have that happen. Your imagination may have a powerful effect on you prior to a public speaking engagement. The same may be true about the thought of asking the opposite sex for a date, worrying what he or she will say in response to your query. Some people won't even start the conversation because of the fear of rejection. Another negative thought.

You can train your imagination to work in your favor. Think of any famous athlete in any sport, when the game is on the line, the great ones always want the ball. As winners, they welcome the pressure and live for it.

There are two out, bottom of the ninth, bases loaded, and you're up by a run. You're playing short-stop, watching your pitcher wind up to throw the pitch. A winner is thinking, "Hit the ball to me, I'll throw him out," not, "I hope he hits it to someone else."

The winner expects to make the play, just like the top players in the N.B.A. expect to make that shot at the buzzer to win the game. Missing it doesn't enter their minds. It's been said that winners make things happen and losers let things happen. Ask yourself what *you* would be thinking. Are you concentrating more on success or failure?

Interviews involving top race car drivers are all pretty much the same. Prior to the race, they all imagine themselves driving flawlessly around the track, leading and winning the race. They don't dwell on the negatives, like mechanical problems, or worse, having an accident. In fact, most of them say when you start thinking more about accidents than winning it is probably time to quit.

Successful people, whether we are talking about sports, business, or life, have many things in common. Most importantly of which is the development of a winning attitude. They are positive thinkers and have learned how to program their minds with the power of positive imagination. They see themselves making those great plays, not failing at them. The word failure doesn't exist to them. They are the epitome of self-confidence. In short, they are playing to win, not just trying to keep from losing.

Understand your mind can be your number one ally, or it can be your biggest enemy. It's all up to you. Your mind stands at the ready to retrieve whatever you decide. For example, if you look at a task and think, I *can't* do it, your mind will go into its memory bank and begin pulling out all of the reasons why you are right. It will remind you of all the times that you tried the same thing, or something like it before, and failed miserably. Another part of your brain will back this up by telling you that you are crazy to even think of trying this again!

The opposite is also true. If you looked at the same task and thought, I *can* do it, your mind will again begin pulling out reasons why you are right. Your mind will remind you of those experiences when you were a great success, and your brain gets in the act again by telling you that you can do this, and there is no way you can fail.

What Henry Ford said is so true, "If you think you can, or if you think you can't, you're right."

I can't overemphasize the importance of positive programming. People who say, "I don't program negatives," just did. Instead of "I don't program negatives," try "I program positives."

Many who feel they aren't programming negatives probably are, if they are watching the eleven o'clock news and then going straight to bed before they have a chance to turn around the negatives they absorbed from the broadcast. Don't let your day begin or end with negatives.

Decide now to improve your life. If you want to take a step toward becoming more self-confident, start by building confidence in what you already know.

If you are in sales, and you have made a sale at least once, all you have to do is recreate the situation, and with it, the feeling that you had in your mind when you made that sale. By doing this you are building on a positive. You know you have done it once, so you can do it again and again. Celebrate, relive, and learn from your successes. Also learn from your failures, because if you don't, they were for nothing. Ask yourself what went wrong and why. Then determine how it *will* be better next time. Not how you hope it doesn't happen again. How it **WILL** be better! With this accomplished, move on. Don't continue to dwell on failure or you'll never get started again.

Learn to accentuate the positive. Look back at trophies, plaques, and awards and recall how you felt when things were going great. But what if you have never accomplished anything in your life? I doubt this is the case, but even if it is, you can still "relive" your great experiences.

To continue the sales example, you can start by envisioning the making of a sale and having everything go perfectly. Your subconscious cannot tell the difference between something that has actually happened and something that has been fabricated.

This is why you hear of people who are about to speak before a group, or are about to perform, "seeing" themselves doing very well before it ever takes place. It's the power of positive programming.

# CHAPTER SEVEN

# SELF-CONFIDENCE...
# DON'T LEAVE HOME WITHOUT IT

We have been discussing the mental side of positive programming, but what can we do to exhibit a positive attitude, in short, radiate self-confidence?

Self-confidence is the reaction to positive programming. However, it is important to differentiate between self-confidence and egotism, as they are seen by some as one in the same. How often have you heard people say, "It's not bragging if it's true" or "It's not bragging if you can do it." Well let's face it folks, it's bragging. Being self-confident means you know how good you are and you don't have to tell everyone. Self-confidence means letting your actions speak for your ability, because if you're as good as you believe, others will brag for you. Most people who spend a great deal of time telling me how great they are, really seem to be trying to convince themselves more than me.

However, most people don't have a bragging problem, they have a self-confidence problem. What is self-confidence? It's asking your boss for a raise, knowing you deserve it based on your performance. It's knowing you have the ability to succeed and overcome anything life throws your way. It's the feeling that you deserve not only what you have and where you are in life, but the next step too!

How do you feel when you are around confident people? Do you feel uplifted? Do you get a little more charged up about life? Do people feel that way around you?

Self-confident people are attractive to most of us because they make us feel better. Those lacking in self-confidence may wish they could be like the self-confident "attractive" people but may not know where to start.

Following is a list of items I believe will help us move our positive programming into action.

1.) Believe in yourself.

This is old news at this point in the book, but it hasn't lost any of its importance. For people to believe in you, you must believe in yourself first. Believe you will be more confident, that the things you are doing mentally (positive programming) and physically (action) will make a difference. If you don't master this, what follows will be a waste of time.

2.) Get into the habit of greeting people first.

When you are at a party, convention, seminar, or any gathering of people, be first to extend your hand and introduce yourself. This may be tough at the beginning if you're not used to it, but it gets easier with practice. It's very important not to do this unconsciously. By this I mean, after the person walks away, you find you're asking yourself, "What was their name?" or "Did I even tell them my name?" Which brings us to...

3.) Greet people properly.

There is a right way to meeting people that many of us may take for granted because we have been doing it all of our lives. First, while making eye contact, extend your hand and accompany it with a big smile. Eye contact is very important because most of us don't trust (even if only subconsciously) someone who won't look us in the eye when they are talking to us. Eye contact shows self-confidence by exhibiting you have nothing to hide. As for smiling, it not only puts the other person more at ease, it also makes you feel better. Many people say they are happy, but you would never know it by looking at their face.

Second, say your name clearly, so they can understand and remember it. More importantly listen and understand their name. If you didn't hear it clearly ask them to repeat it to make sure you have it right. Many people think this is embarrassing. It's not half as embarrassing as having to introduce your new friend 5 minutes later and not being able to remember his name. Making the effort to get people's names right also shows it is important to you and that certainly doesn't hurt either.

> 4.) Use that person's name when talking to him.

It has been proven that hearing your own name is one of the sweetest sounds you can hear.

> 5.) Be easy to get along with.

Have you ever been around someone and after they left, you felt drained and worn out? It seemed like the conversation was a battle. Whatever you said, they disagreed with or topped in some way. Are you looking forward to your next conversation with this person? Probably not. This tells us to not always try to get in the last word. Relax, being confident doesn't mean you have to always be better or show how much you know.

> 6.) Praise others.

We have already talked about the power of praise, but it warrants another mention here. Give credit where credit is due and remember, praise is fine as long as you are not fishing for a compliment. If that is the motivation for praising someone it is better left unsaid.

> 7.) Practice sounding, looking, and acting confident.

Sound confident in the things you say. Don't say, "I think I can get that accomplished," when what you know and want to say is, "I am sure I can get that completed on time." Don't start a sentence with, "This may sound a little silly," when you know if it really was silly you wouldn't be saying it at all. Say what you mean, come to the point, be consistent, and have a confident tone in your voice.

Looking confident means proper grooming and clothing. Who doesn't feel more confident when they look their best? So why put yourself at a disadvantage? It pays to go first class. It is better to have one good suit, than two bad ones. This is your life we are talking about, don't short change yourself.

Acting confidently means being in control of yourself and your actions. Be in control of yourself with proper body language. Stand up straight, with your head up and your shoulders back. You can spot a person that is depressed or lacks confidence in themselves immediately, without them saying a word, simply by what their body language is telling you.

Be in control of your actions. For instance, if you promise to return someone's call, do it! If you promise to meet someone somewhere, do it! When you promise something to someone, follow through! Be able to deliver! Act the part and act decisively. Stand by your word, because a good reputation can't be purchased for any price, only earned.

The more you act like a winner, the more people will treat you like a winner, which in turn will give you the confidence to do the things you want to do.

Now we are taking steps toward conquering...

# CHAPTER EIGHT

## FEAR...DESTROYER OF DREAMS

It is true that fear kills. It stops people from being their best, and it stops some entirely. There are many types of fear. Fear of rejection, fear of the unknown, fear of failure, and even fear of success, just to name a few.

Let's examine the fear of failure. First we must realize that most of the fears people have today, they have developed. We were not born with a fear of public speaking, or a fear of flying, we have developed these fears ourselves. It stands to reason that if we created these fears, we should be able to overcome them.

We are afraid to try because we might fail. We must learn to look at a situation and ask, "What is the worst thing that could happen?" Many people have a tendency to take every situation, find the worst scenario, then exaggerate it beyond belief. Learn to keep things in perspective.

Realize that fear is our choice. Fear is misplaced conviction. It is believing more strongly that life will defeat you, instead of believing that you possess the ability to conquer life's challenges.

We choose to let what others think, freeze us. The irony to this is that many of those from whom we seek this unspoken approval, are the same people we would not take advice from or want to emulate in the first place.

To be successful, you must get outside your comfort zone. If you are only doing what you're comfortable with, you're probably not growing in life. In order to grow, you must challenge yourself and extend beyond by doing the things that make you slightly uncomfortable.

Again, be aware of the path of least resistance. It is easier to be frozen by fear, than to fight to overcome it. If it was easy, everyone would be doing it.

The two things that kill fear are knowledge and action. Knowledge can be viewed as preparation. First, learn to admit your fears to yourself and set about obtaining the knowledge to overcome them, then take action.

Most will agree that public speaking is a fear many of us share. Surveys have shown that many people feel public speaking is more frightening than death. Even though it has been proven that death is harder on you physically than speaking.

Public speaking was one of my biggest fears and I

decided to overcome it. I had held a real estate license for about eighteen months and a friend suggested I get involved teaching real estate courses. We said earlier that knowledge kills fear. The thought of teaching a class that eighteen months earlier had given me fits as a student, told me that if I decided to go into this, it was going to be a lot of work.

One evening I went to the real estate school to watch an instructor I had particularly enjoyed during my enrollment. He looked like he was having fun and was making the class enjoyable for everyone. I looked around, taking into consideration the size of the room, and the number of people, before asking myself, "Could I do this?" I decided that I could do it, maybe not as well at first, but I *could* do it. Entertaining this thought was easy because I didn't have to leave my seat and I was the only one in the entire room that knew what I was considering.

I went to the school director and asked if he needed instructors, and if so, how could I apply? He asked me if I had ever taught before, or for that matter if I had ever spoken in front of a group before. I said no, but that it was always a goal of mine and that I was willing to work hard at it. He helped to build my confidence by reminding me that if I was to go before a group not properly prepared, they would probably tear my head off. I found this to be a comforting thought.

Needless to say, my credentials were lacking, but we hit it off fairly well from the start, so he decided to give me a chance. He said , "Here is what you will have to do. If you want to be an instructor, get your real estate instructor's license and then sit through three entire real estate courses, each course with a different instructor. Then *if* there is an opening, and I like what I see, you'll get a class of your own to instruct. Of course, you won't be paid for your time spent in training." (He was doing fine until he said that.) "I will notify the front office and you are to log your time with the instructors."

Each course lasted fifty-one hours, and I had already gone through it once to get my salesman's license, but of course that didn't count. His reasoning was, first, you would become very knowledgeable, and second, anyone crazy enough to do this without pay must really want to teach real estate.

After completing all the things he asked, I was ready for my shot at teaching a class, however there weren't any openings. All that I could do was wait. I began to fear that I would forget some of the things that I had learned, so occasionally I went to the school on nights when I could find an empty room, and practiced "projecting information."

By now my fear had turned into fire. I was so ready to do this that I couldn't stand it. There I was, licensed, with over 200 training hours, and no place to teach.

Well, the night finally came for me to teach a class. I was ready, or so I thought. I was in the office waiting for the registrars to check everyone in as the classroom kept filling up. When everyone had checked in, I was advised that I could start. I told myself that I had done my homework, I was prepared, this is what I had worked for, so let's go do it.

I opened the classroom door at the back of the room and saw what appeared to be a million people. I immediately closed the door. The only problem was that I was still outside. What I felt next was frightening. Increased heart rate, sweaty palms, and my chest felt like it was in a vice that was slowly closing around me.

For the first time in my life I understood the full meaning of stage fright. I also understood why some would rather die than talk in front of a group. I told myself that if I could do this, I could do anything. It didn't help. I had about one minute to turn this around, because not only were there over one hundred students in the room, there was one school director waiting in there also.

I had to talk myself up. I had worked my butt off learning this material, they didn't. I was prepared, I had the knowledge, and after all they didn't know it was my first class. I decided I wasn't going to die, that if I just got started, it would flow.

Zig Ziglar says, "If you don't like public speaking, don't do it. Stick to private speaking." What he is saying is finding those friendly faces in the crowd and direct your talk toward them. That is what I decided to do.

I was right, I didn't die. In fact I liked it so much I continued to teach evenings for almost eight years. This ultimately led to the seminars I am presenting today.

The bottom line is, everyone has fears. The difference is, the people who succeed are able to work through their fears to accomplish their goals. That is a definition of courage.

Do what you fear most and fear will vanish. It doesn't happen overnight, but if you want something badly enough, you can obtain it. Never let your fears stop you from doing the things that you truly want to do.

# CHAPTER NINE

# GOING FOR IT

We have all heard someone say, "Go for it!" We may have even said it ourselves. However, few people ever really go for it. Imagine the drive it takes to be an Olympian. Your goal is four or more years away and everything you do between now and the Olympics is set on one goal, winning the gold medal. Olympians epitomize drive, determination, positive attitude, will to win, and the ability to be focused on a goal. In short, everything it takes to win.

A number of years ago Olympic hopefuls were interviewed and asked this question. If you had a choice, which would you select? Winning a gold medal in your sport and only living one year after that, or not winning, and having the opportunity to live out your normal life. More than half chose winning and only living one more year. If that doesn't show focus, determination, and the will to win, nothing does.

I have never seen a professional fighter that didn't totally believe that he was going to win the fight. Their confidence is unshakable. I doubt that you have ever seen a negative thinking fighter. What trouble they would be in if they took the attitude of some of the people we meet everyday! Let's see how it sounds. Here is a fictitious pre-fight interview.

Interviewer: "Tell us how you are feeling about today's fight, Bob."

Fighter: "O.K., I guess."

Interviewer: "I mean do you feel ready, prepared to take the title? Are you going to knock him out?"

Fighter: "I'm not really sure if I can win or not, I'm just going to show up and see what happens."

With this attitude can you guess what is going to happen? Right! He is going to get destroyed. We look at the above conversation and say that it is ridiculous if the guy really wants to win. We expect a fighter to say things like, "I feel great, I've trained hard, and I'm ready for a big victory. There is no way that I'm going to be denied."

But how many people do you know that always answer, "How do you feel or how is it going?" with, "O.K., I guess." How many people just "show up" to see what happens? Like the fighter, if we want to be champions we have to show up with a positive attitude and expect to win.

Some people can't relate to this kind of focus because they don't feel like they are in the "do or die" situations that these athletes experience.

We may not be performing in the spotlight as they are, but our inability to focus on a goal can be just as devastating over the long term.

Fortunately, our success does not always depend on us facing the best in our profession every time we compete. You can't win them all and fortunately, we don't have to in order to succeed. We just need to win our share. You can win your share merely by showing up, having a positive attitude, and expecting to be successful. Imagine how you would feel if whenever you made a mistake on your job, it was broadcast on the evening news, picturing you along with an instant replay of your mistake. Sound ridiculous? Football players must endure this when they make mistakes on the field. Politicians are scrutinized more closely today than ever, and everything, good as well as bad, is splattered in the news for all to see. It's a good thing our mistakes are a little more private.

So why don't we go for it? Because someone will think it is silly? Because someone told you that you would fail anyway? Because someone will think you're crazy? Ask yourself, "What do I have to lose?" Many years ago, before I invested in my first investment property, my biggest fear was going broke if I slipped up and made a bad investment. A good friend of mine cured me with one line.  He said, "I don't know why you are afraid of going broke, you are already broke!" That was when I first asked myself, "What do I have to lose?"

Most people today are afraid to get "out of step" and are scared to try something new.  They don't realize that it is this type of attitude that is probably holding them back from something great. So they do the same things everyday and get deeper and deeper into a rut. This continues until they are so far down in this rut, that they can no longer see any options, only barriers ironically created by themselves. In a way it is like being in prison, but with a peculiar twist. They are the ones who have the key to unlock the door to freedom, but choose not to use it.

In life, if you don't choose a direction, one will be chosen for you.  Usually by someone who no longer has any dreams, and has probably tried to keep you from dreaming too. As we said earlier, never let anyone, especially those who haven't made it, stop you from making it. It is not like you are being threatened by bodily harm. Mere words usually stop many from competing today, spoken by those who have never learned to go for it themselves.

Going after what you want is a little like eating an elephant. You can't eat it in one bite, and achieving your lifelong goals cannot be achieved instantly either. However, you can do it one bite, or one step, at a time.

The important thing is the realization that while few can stay motivated for as long as it takes to win, most can stay motivated for 30, 60, or 90 days. So "energize" towards all of your long term goals by going for it in increments of 30, 60, or 90 days.

Pretend that after a set period, some fictitious world rule will take effect that will stop you from continuing forever your efforts in that chosen direction. For example, if you are trying to save money, pretend that after 90 days, no more money will be allowed to be saved. So you need to make a big effort to save for the next 90 days. If you are trying to build a sales force, pretend that you wouldn't be allowed to hire any new salespeople after the next 90 days.

While you know this isn't true, what you have done is create a fictitious sense of urgency that will help you to accomplish your goals. After reaching your goal, reward yourself, and start another 90 day time frame.

Get into the habit of putting your motivational surges into 30, 60, and 90 day periods and reward yourself when you achieve your accomplishments. Learn to be tough on yourself when you fall short. Be fair but be firm.

Now that you're ready to go for it, we are prepared to talk about the art of ...

# CHAPTER TEN

# SETTING GOALS THAT WIN

Imagine for a moment, that you stepped up to a ticket counter at an airport and said, "One ticket, please." The attendant responds, "To where?" To which you reply, "I don't know." Sounds a little ridiculous, doesn't it? Does it sound like something that you, or someone you know would ever do? Probably not.

However, many people do the equivalent of this every day. They go through life without any goals or plans and don't have any idea where they are going, but somehow expect everything to work out just fine. Would you agree that you are probably not going to wind up in your dream location if you have no plans or road map to help you get there?

How would you feel, if after being airborne for an hour, your pilot says that he is trying something new; he is going to find the city at which you are supposed to land without the use of maps or navigational equipment. He tells you that he is just going to fly around until he finds what he is looking for. This pilot has a goal, but no plan of how to get there.

From this example, I think you would agree that just having an ultimate goal is not enough, unless you have the map to go with it. The "map" is a series of smaller goals that take you on your journey to success. Once we have our dream, proper goal setting will show us how to attain it.

First, your goals should be in three groups: short, intermediate, and long. Short term is one to six months, intermediate one to three years, and long term five years or longer. Following is a list of items to be used as a guideline of what goals must be.

1.) Goals must be envisioned.

Know exactly what you want. Because let's face it, if you don't, how will you ever attain it? You must be able to see yourself actually being or possessing whatever your goal was originally. Get into the envisioning habit several times a day. You are halfway to any goal if you can "see" yourself achieving it first.

2.) Have a passionate desire to achieve your goals.

If all you do is make a list of things that would be "nice" to accomplish, forget it! In order to achieve our goals we must have a burning desire to do so. When I was leading a sales organization, I would have always rather had one person with a burning desire to succeed, than a great number of people who only had an interest in success.

3.) Make your goals well-defined and measurable.

Know what you want. Be specific and make sure your short term goals allow you to measure your progress. I am going to be a better salesperson or I'm going to get into better shape are examples of abstract, immeasurable goals. You may make progress in these areas but it won't seem like it because it can't be measured. In order to make the above goals measurable you would first determine what would make you a better salesperson, (taking certain courses, earning certain designations, etc.) or what you would have to do to be in better shape, (specific exercise program, specific diet, exact number of pounds you want to lose, etc.) Then you will have your "road map" goals in place for success. You should be able to check often as to where you stand on your road to success. Check and/ or re-assess your goals about every six months to see if they are getting you closer or taking you farther away from your ultimate objectives.

4.) Be flexible.

Be ready to re-adjust your goals and not give up on them. If they are too easy they won't be worthwhile, and if they are too tough, the "goals are

71

stupid" attitude can creep in. Remember, small victories lead to big successes.

5.) Your goals must be attainable.

It isn't realistic to believe that anybody can do anything they want. Even if I was armed with the most positive attitude in the world, I doubt very much if I could become Heavyweight Champion of the World in boxing. I say this because I have never weighed over 165 pounds in my life, and with a build like mine, all I am going to survive is the weigh-in. Your goals must be attainable, and most importantly *you* must believe that you can reach them. *You* can achieve whatever you can believe.

6.) Set your own goals.

You must set your own goals, not let others set them for you. Goals set by others for you are not usually the same ones that you would set for yourself, therefore you aren't as motivated to achieve them as you would your own.

7.) Goals need to have a definite time period.

If you don't believe this, look around at all the things you have been meaning to do for a long time, but have never done. You had the goals, but no time frame to complete them.

8.) Write down your goals.

If you don't, your likelihood of achieving

them is drastically reduced.  Look what happens when we go grocery shopping without our list.  Do we forget some of the items?  Do we accomplish our goals of getting everything that we wanted originally?

9.) Take action.

This is the most important one of all.  Have you ever made New Year's resolutions that have gone unfulfilled?  What good is it to make them if you don't take action?

Don't think for a minute that just selecting a few things that you might like, constitutes proper goal setting.  That is called wishing, not goal setting.  Remember to follow the proper steps.

It has been said that most people don't plan to fail, they just fail to plan.  A person without goals is a person without a game plan, and that person is doomed to drift through life like a ship without a rudder, directionless.  Once you have your road map, all that is left is to take action and follow through.

# CHAPTER ELEVEN

## TIME CONTROL

Did you ever sit down at the end of a day and wonder where it went? It seems like you were very busy, but it also seems like you didn't get much accomplished. Well you are not alone. We have all felt like that at some time or another.

Do you realize that many people spend more time planning their family vacation, than they do planning their everyday lives or for that matter their future?

"Spending time" is something we all do whether we want to or not. Some spend time carefully, others carelessly, but we are all forced to spend it at the same constant rate, sixty minutes per hour, hour after hour, day after day.

Most of us say we don't have enough time, but since none of us can get any more, we must do the next best thing. Become better time managers and learn to control time instead of letting it control us.

Time is a resource that must be spent wisely. Realize that whatever you do better be important to you, because you are exchanging a part of your life for it. You must take control of time before you can take control of your life, and even though you cannot get back lost time, it is never too late to start investing time wisely. Because if you're not investing it, you're wasting it.

The way to do this is to focus on daily and weekly schedules and follow them. Plan your day. Draw up "must do" and "should do" lists daily with at least 3-5 items under each, and carry it with you. For those who find it difficult to fit this in, start by taking a four week period and don't do anything differently than you do now. However, start a diary, and for this period of time record everything you do hourly. You will be amazed at how much time is wasted everyday. From this you can determine where changes need to be made, and then you can implement your new schedule.

Avoid time takers, people who are willing to just "shoot the breeze" and accomplish nothing. Don't dwell on problems as most will go away without your help, or in spite of it. Work toward solutions.

How would you like to be able to have one month a year that you could use to study or learn new things, go to seminars, and in general just use to build your mind?

You can! If you spend at least 45 minutes in your car every day, you are spending more than a month of eight hour days in your car every year. You could be using that time to learn information from cassettes. This is a great way to build knowledge while you are driving. These tapes can be of prominent speakers or of notes that you have recorded for your own review. Learn to make use of "down" time.

Another example of "down" time is time wasted waiting in line. How much time do we spend a year sitting in doctors offices, barber shops, or just waiting for others? Having a pocket recorder or note pad handy can help us maximize this wasted time by using it to plan or schedule other parts of our lives.

A car phone is another way to improve productivity. Being able to conduct business while you are driving is a great asset. I have noticed that I spend less time "just talking" and more time handling business when I am using the car phone because each minute costs money.

Try handling all of your business calls the same way when you're on a regular phone, as if they cost you by the minute, because in a different way, they do! You may be surprised to see how much time is saved on each call.

Also, we can certainly learn from others regarding time management, by avoiding time takers and time wasters and copying those who invest time wisely.

Lastly, be where you are! If you are somewhere physically, but not mentally, it's just like not being there at all. Have you ever been at a seminar and had so many things on your mind that you learned virtually nothing? You wasted your money, but more importantly you wasted your time. Money you can get back; however, lost time can never be retrieved.

Remember, we all have 24 hours in a day to work with, and it is how intelligently that we use them that will determine our degree of success in life. Resolve to start making the most of this precious commodity today.

# CHAPTER TWELVE

# CALLING YOUR OWN SHOTS

When we talk about going for it, from the standpoint of business, most of us have two choices. Either climb the corporate ladder or be our own boss.

Working for corporate America has its good and bad points. Some of the positives are usually security, benefits, and consistent pay. However, these are the same things that have a tendency to put today's corporate worker in a box. The bottom of the box is the minimum the company will pay, and the top is the maximum. They really don't pay the employee, they pay the position through the use of guidelines. You are kept in this box by side walls known as benefits. For many, this concept is fine, but for most it is not.

Understand, even though it may not be fine for them, they do it anyway, conditioned by others as the way it is supposed to be.

If you were told that a good job, college degree, and loyalty would equal success, you were probably mislead. Most of us would agree that we would rather own a house than rent one. Even if it meant repairs, mowing the lawn, etc. The reason is because after all those years of payments, you have something. The alternative? A fist full of rent receipts.

The same people who believe in owning instead of renting a house, rent instead of own their lives. By working for someone else, they are helping to build equity for a company that is not theirs, just like renting a home.

How would you have felt, if, on your first day of work, your boss called you into his office and told you the kind of car you would have to buy, the kind of house you would have to live in, and determined which college your children were going to attend? You would probably say that you wouldn't put up with that. You would probably say that you would make your own choices. But do you? Or does your boss really make these decisions based on how much he pays you?

John Paul Getty once said, "Going to work for a large company is like getting on a train. Are you going sixty miles an hour, or is the train going sixty miles an hour and you're just sitting still?"

I believe a person is a success if they are able to

do what they want, **when** they want. If you always wanted to own a gas station, and one day you buy one, you are a success to the most important person in the world, you. If you always longed for a job in the corporate world, and finally got one doing what you want, you would be a success. If however, you are working for someone else and long to be your own boss, then you still have work to do to become successful. If you are just going through the motions, then you're in a rut, and it has been said that that resembles a grave.

Here is a short test to see if you are going through the motions.

1) Do you say "Thank God it's Friday?"

2) Have you stopped dreaming and are now just surviving?

3) Do you have Sunday night blues? (That is the feeling most of us had as kids when we knew we had school the next day, and have now, knowing we have to go to work the next day.)

4) If someone asks how you are at the start of a week, do you respond with, "O.K., for a Monday?"

5) Do you endure Monday through Friday, just to get to the weekend; or put another way, are you throwing away over 70% of your life to live what's left?

If you answered one or more of these questions affirmatively, you are probably in a rut. It is no secret that most people do not like what they are doing for a living. They are not really living, they are surviving. But their need for security is so strong, they are willing to do what makes them unhappy, to have it. They are not playing to win, they are trying to avoid losing. Will Rogers once said, "Lord, let me live until I'm dead." The question is, are *you* living or just surviving?

Recently I heard a radio interview with a former personnel manager, who was responsible for hiring employees for a large company. He said their company used to advertise for people with initiative and drive, but really wanted people who didn't possess those qualities, so they would fit into the corporate mold and not rock the boat. There is no dress rehearsal in life. One of the saddest things to see, is at a retirement party, where someone who has worked their entire life, now wishes they had taken that chance to have started their own business, or made that career change when the opportunity had presented itself. Are you on the same track? Envision yourself now at retirement. Are you satisfied with your life? If not, then now is the time to change.

I believe you can start this change by asking yourself better questions. Instead of, "Why me?" and "Why now?" learn to ask, "Why not me?" and "Why not today?" We only get to go around once, so we have to make the most of it. What would you try if you were guaranteed success in advance and failure was not an option? Why not try it? Why not today? Learn to dream again. What a shame it is for those who don't.

# CHAPTER THIRTEEN

# CARE AND MAINTENANCE

This chapter is one that carries as much, if not more, weight than any of the others in this book. The reason is because you can have a winning attitude and be striving to reach your goals, but without your health, the completion or enjoyment of these goals becomes almost, if not entirely impossible.

You don't have to be in absolute top physical condition to enjoy the fruits of your labor, just being in "good" shape will do.

I want to preface what I am about to say, by telling you that I am not a nutritionist or a doctor. I simply want to share with you things that I feel are common sense regarding staying in good shape. What follows has worked very well for me.

So what is "good" shape? Attain your proper weight, don't smoke, don't drink alcohol, eat the right foods, and get the right amount of sleep. "That's all," you say?

This will be easier for some than it will be for others. Many may think this could take a long time to turn around. This may be true but it did take most people a long time to pick up these bad habits.

None us were born smoking cigarettes, drinking alcohol, or eating junk food. It's true that many people start out with good intentions, however many end up being programmed by those around them.

We may have started out playing sports and being active, but as we grew older, working became a big part of our lives and for many of us the time we spent exercising and staying in shape has evaporated.

Almost everyone that has been fortunate enough to be relatively healthy has taken their health for granted. We forget that good health is something that has to be maintained and that without our health we have nothing.

Not surprisingly, most pet owners treat their pets better than they treat themselves. When you think about it, most pets eat well, get plenty of sleep, and very few drink alcohol or smoke.

Let's talk about smoking for a moment. I've never met anyone who didn't think smoking wasn't bad, even those who smoke. If you smoke, think back to that first cigarette. Was it as easy to smoke as the one you had this morning? Probably not. More than likely your body tried to tell you with that very first cigarette that it wasn't a good idea by making you cough. You were able to survive that, by smoking enough cigarettes until your body accepted this as the way it was going to be.

I have a good friend who was overweight. He decided he needed to make additional money, so he got involved working part-time at night. What he discovered was that his excess weight took away a lot of his energy and made it difficult for him to work the extra hours. He decided that he needed to lose weight if he was going to continue with this part-time endeavor and that is exactly what he did. He has recently completed a professionally supervised weight loss program and now finds that he has more energy than he ever imagined.

Most people fail at dieting because they don't understand one simple concept. That is, for most, proper weight control comes from making proper eating and exercising habits a way of life, not a once in a while thing that you do until you drop the few pounds that you want to lose. Many people will diet, improperly, (e.g.; starve themselves) and as soon as they have lost the weight they wanted, go right back to their old habits. A good eating and exercise program should be an "all the time" thing. This doesn't mean that you shouldn't splurge once in a while, however the key word here is moderation. To put it simply, if you take in more calories than you burn up, you are going to get fat!

And now a word about exercise. Here it is: CAUTION. If you're over 30, or overweight, start slowly and/or get a doctor's approval first. Don't try to get into shape all at once. Remember, you probably didn't get out of shape all at once either. A lot of people say they don't have time to exercise. They may have less time if they don't.

Find simple ways to sneak exercise into your daily routine. For instance, when appropriate, walk instead of drive and take the stairs instead of using the elevator. Learn to ask yourself, "What have I done this week to improve my health?"

So far we have been discussing only half of the health picture, the physical half. The mental side is equally important.

By mental half I mean taking time to "smell the roses." Take the time to schedule relaxation, just as you would appointments and stick to it. Spend time doing things with your friends and family. Spend time improving your life outside of business. Invest in recreation. These things are important in helping you avoid "burnout."

Also learn to control stress. No one can control stress until they realize that controlling it is a decision that is totally yours. You choose stress everyday by the way you react to a given situation. Remember, nothing has meaning except that which you attach to it. Things are only as good or as bad as you perceive.

Take driving a car. Could this be a potentially stressful situation? You bet! See if this sounds familiar. It's Monday morning, and you are late for work. You jump into your car, head down the road, and promptly miss the first three traffic lights. Just when you start to make up some time, you wind up behind two retired drivers, each in his own lane, having a slow race. You begin asking yourself questions. "Don't these people have something else they could be doing? Why do old people have to be on the road at this time anyway? What is so important, that can't wait until after rush hour?" Rush hour, now there is a term that lends itself to calm and peacefulness.

Suddenly it is everyone else's fault that you are going to be late for work. The fact that you got up late is long forgotten. Meanwhile these two old folks cause you to miss another light, and this one only takes a couple of hours to turn green. When you are in a hurry, they all take that long to change. Actually, the only times that I remember lights changing quickly, are when I am trying to find a location on a road map, or trying to refold a road map! Anyway, the light turns green and you swear that they are both asleep at the wheel. You hit the horn. Finally, one of them finds the gas pedal. You make a quick lane change and miss another light. After what seems like a week later, you arrive at work, only to find that your boss is off today.

You smile to yourself and think you got away with something. But, in reality, you didn't. Because all of the morning's aggravation has taken its toll on you physically. This is a scenario that could have been easily avoided simply by getting up and leaving home earlier.

But what about the times when the situation is outside your control? Let's change the above example slightly. You are driving to work and you're ahead of schedule. As you are going down the road, someone cuts you off. How do *you* react?

When you get upset, it usually means that you already had some anger built up inside of you. You may not be able to control all of the situations around you, but you can control your reactions. For many, controlling their reactions means controlling or alleviating the anger inside of them.

Try to imagine your reaction to the above scenario, if that morning, before you got into your car, someone handed you $1,000,000. Are you a little less apt to chew through your seat belt? Probably. But what was the difference? Same situation, same drivers, different attitude. You received $1,000,000 this morning and his/her actions on the road didn't hold the same meaning.

There will always be times when things will happen that will make you angry. Sometimes you may think, "Someday I'll look back on this and laugh." Well, do it now! Don't wait until later to find the humor in it. Find it now! Laugh now! Remember it is all a mindset. You choose your reactions. So choose a happy one, one without stress.

If you can't find anything funny in a bad situation, at least minimize it, or reduce it. Try taking the situation and comparing it to the size of the universe. Suddenly, it doesn't seem like such a big problem. The problem hasn't changed, the universe hasn't changed, but your way of looking at the problem has, and that's what is important.

Situations in life are constantly being produced, and your ability to act in a positive way determines how much self-induced stress you will have to endure.

Learn to stop worrying; first it doesn't solve problems, and secondly, it has been proven that most of the things people worry about have either already happened or won't happen at all. Emotional control may be something that doesn't come easy, but it is a skill that can be acquired, and can add years to your life.

# CHAPTER FOURTEEN

# SIMPLE GUIDELINES FOR
# BEING FINANCIALLY FIT

A lot of people wondered why I decided to put a chapter regarding investments, in a book about positive mental attitude. I have two reasons for this decision. First, it takes some of the same qualities to succeed at financial wealth as it does to succeed mentally at life. By this I mean positive attitude, planning, goal setting, etc. Secondly, while I don't believe that money is the most important thing in life, it is way up there, and what good is a positive attitude if you end up in poverty, like many Americans do today, living off of friends or the government.

If you don't believe that people end up this way, look around you. People today are still working late in life because they need the money to survive. I believe it is because no one ever told them how to win at the game of proper retirement. Do you realize that you will probably earn a fortune during your lifetime and yet the odds are you will be broke when you retire?

For most of us, our first try at money management was receiving an allowance when we were kids. How did you do with it? Did you learn to save for what you wanted or were you always borrowing on credit, that is getting an advance from Mom and Dad? If you are like most of us, you can see some similarities between then and now. First, it never seemed like we had enough money, and second, we were always living on credit. Fortunately, my Mom and Dad never charged me interest or made me put up collateral, at least not at age 6. (That started three years later!) However, like most banks, they didn't always say yes.

But that was then, so let's try a little game to see how we have done with the allowance we have been receiving since.

First, let's figure our net worth. This is something that you should do quarterly. Start by listing all of your assets on one side of the page, such as the value of your home, car, savings, stocks, etc. On the other side of the page, list your liabilities, mortgage, car loan, credit card balance, in short, all monies owed. Now all you have to do is subtract. The result is your net worth.

If you assume that your working life is from ages 25-65, and you are 45 now, you are half-way to retirement. How does your net worth stack up against all the money you have earned? If you are like most, you are surprised and you are wondering where the money went.

Let's take a look at the average American. Even if he makes $30,000 per year and never gets a raise, he will earn $1.2 million in his lifetime. The odds are now that he will wind up with approximately $10,000 in the bank at retirement.

This is when the law of justification takes over. People will begin to justify why they don't have the things in life that they wanted. For instance, there is no reason to vacation in Europe, when you consider the dangers of traveling abroad today. There is no reason to have a nice sports car, because it is not practical. We don't need a newer or nicer home, because moving is such a pain. It is certainly not because they cannot afford it.

The real shame is that by proper planning and by following some simple guidelines they could have afforded it. They could have retired in dignity.

If our young people today are being trained by people with these statistics, where do you believe they are likely to end up?

I believe people fail at financial success, not because it is difficult to understand, but because no one ever taught us these simple principles. All through high school and college, no one ever showed us what to do with all of the money we were going to be making from the good jobs we would be getting, as a result of being in school in the first place. This still hasn't changed today. The few "finance" classes that are being taught today, are almost always, if not always, being taught by people who are not financially independent. (See chapter four, line one, "People can't lead you where they haven't been.")

It is not my intention in this chapter to go into great detail regarding investments. It is, however, my desire to share with you simple guidelines that have helped me become financially fit.

Because of the fact that we are just scratching the surface in this chapter, I am advising that you take whatever information applies to you, and research it thoroughly to make the most of it in your own personal situation.

To start with, I believe in paying yourself first. Most people have too much month left at the end of the money, so if they wait until all the bills are paid to start putting savings away, they probably never will. A good amount to pay yourself is ten percent. Take that off the top and save it. If you can afford to save more than that, great! Save for a rainy day, regardless of current weather conditions. Saving should be a habit, not something you do until you have enough to buy your next toy.

Next, live below your means. Most have a problem with this one too. The more they make, the more they spend. This usually continues until they are making great money, but still don't have their retirement nest-egg built. What they have is more expensive toys and bigger payments.

Always look to cut your expenses. Make a log of all expenses for three months. This will show you where all the money is going. Three months is a good time frame because many of us may have some expenditures that are paid quarterly, and this will make sure that we catch them on our log. Savings that we find here can go into our nest egg.

While you are building your retirement account, hold your purchases of depreciating assets to a minimum. You probably need a car, but you don't need the best. You don't need a boat, especially if you haven't bought a home yet. Which brings us to our next point, buying a home. Unless you are thinking about moving soon, this should be one of your top goals. As explained in an earlier chapter, it takes more knowledge than money.

While building your nest egg, it is important that it is growing properly. It is not enough to work hard for money, it must work hard for you.

Understand the rule of 72. The rule of 72 will tell you approximately how long it will take your money to

double at a given interest rate, simply by dividing the
number 72 by that interest rate. For example, money
growing at 6% will double every twelve years, (72
divided by 6 = 12) while money growing at 12%
doubles every six years, (72 divided by 12 = 6.) Doesn't
sound like a big deal? Consider the following. A one
time investment of $1,000 from age 29 to retirement
(65.)

|  | Return 6% |  | Return 12% |
|---|---|---|---|
| Age |  |  |  |
| 29 | $ 1,000 | 29 | $ 1,000 |
| 41 | $ 2,000 | 35 | $ 2,000 |
| 53 | $ 4,000 | 41 | $ 4,000 |
| 65 | $ 8,000 | 47 | $ 8,000 |
|  |  | 53 | $16,000 |
|  |  | 59 | $32,000 |
|  |  | 65 | $64,000 |

WOW! Doubling the interest equals eight times
the money! If you still fail to see the power of this,
allow me to say it in a different way. Let's say you are
age 29, and have a goal of attaining a million dollars 36
years from now at age 65. You are saving in the bank at
6%. Your monthly payment to reach that million dollar
mark is $656. One day you are outside telling your
neighbor, ( who also happens to be 29 ) about your plan

to have a million dollars at retirement. He tells you he is doing the same thing, however it is only costing him $138. How do you feel? What is the only difference in these two examples? Your neighbor is saving at 12%. I know I don't have to ask which makes the most sense.

The rule of 72 gives you a good idea of how powerful the compounding of money can be. Moral: Make sure your money is working at least as hard as you are working.

One of the ways to do this is by eliminating the middleman. Two of the best examples of middlemen today are savings institutions and life insurance companies.

Let's take a moment to look at life insurance. First, keep in mind, life insurance is basically income protection. If you are married with a family, you have responsibility. If your income was to stop due to a premature death, and this would put your family in financial difficulty, you should have life insurance.

Life insurance can be broken down into two categories; term and cash value. The type that is the simplest to understand is term insurance. You pay for a certain "term" and if you pass away during that time a specified sum of money is paid to your beneficiary. Term insurance does not build cash value (savings) and for some, this is the best choice.

However, just as "one size fits all" is known to be one of the biggest misrepresentations of all time, so it is with the idea that everyone who needs life insurance should buy term. But, if as previously mentioned we are looking to eliminate the middleman, then building a retirement in most types of cash value life insurance is something to avoid. Although, there is one type of cash value insurance that does have merit, and that is variable life insurance.

Do your homework and shop around! Not all term insurance is created equal. The same can be said for variable life insurance.

One last comment about life insurance, it's not for everybody. Remember, if no one would be harmed financially by your death, then you probably don't need it at all.

The other middleman I try to eliminate is the savings institution. I believe it is all right to have a small amount of savings in the bank for the little day to day emergencies, however the bulk of my *short term* savings would be in a money-market fund. I don't mean an insured money fund at the bank, as it is not the same thing. Also, I don't believe in putting money into certificates of deposit, or better stated, certificates of depreciation. The reason is because after taxes, they usually don't keep pace with inflation, and there is usually a penalty for taking your money out early.

Another way that I have my money working hard for me is through stock mutual fund investing. The money that I put into a mutual fund is for *longer term* investing. This is money that I won't touch for at least 3-5 years.

The reason I chose that time frame is because, mutual funds are "the market" and the market fluctuates. If you invested money here that you need next month, it could be worth less than when you deposited it and you would have to sell at a loss. Historically, three years and longer is a good time frame to come out ahead if you pick good funds. Remember, mutual funds are not a guaranteed return, but to me that's good. Because a guaranteed rate of return guarantees me that I won't make any more than that given rate.

I have my own simple rules for mutual fund investing that have worked well for me. Let me say that mutual funds are not for everybody, but if this sounds like something for you, do your homework.

1. Normally buy from large fund families.
2. Buy funds that have a good track record, usually a minimum of a five year history.
3. Invest, don't speculate. This means be in for the long term, usually 3-5 years or longer.
4. Dollar cost average your fund investments.

I think all of the above are self-explanatory with the possible exception of number 4. Dollar averaging is a systematic monthly investment as opposed to just putting down a large sum all at once at the beginning. Even though you should still win long term, you don't know whether your share price is at a high or low. If it is at a high and the market drops, it would take a while to get back to even. If you are dollar averaging, you aren't as concerned because if the market drops you are getting more shares for your investment.

Let's look at the following examples:

### (A)    LUMP SUM INVESTING

| Month | Investment | Share price | Shares purchased |
|-------|-----------|-------------|------------------|
| 1     | $300      | $100        | 3                |
| 2     | -         | $1          | 0                |
| 3     | -         | $5          | 0                |
| Total | $300      | -           | 3                |

The value of this account is $15 (3 shares x the closing price of $5 per share.) "Mutual fund investing looks great," you say? Now let's take the same basic numbers and dollar average them.

## (B)   DOLLAR COST AVERAGING

| Month | Investment | Share price | Shares purchased |
|-------|-----------|-------------|------------------|
| 1 | $100 | $100 | 1 |
| 2 | $100 | $1 | 100 |
| 3 | $100 | $5 | 20 |
| | ----------- | ----------- | ----------- |
| Total | $300 | - | 121 |

The value of this account is $605 (121 shares  x the closing price of $5 per share.)

While the market has never dropped like this, and these examples are exaggerated, you can readily see that you still doubled your money when you dollar averaged. This is because you were able to buy more shares for the same investment dollar since the price per share was less. This obviously brings down your average share price.

However, if you buy into a fund, and the market does nothing but decline, neither dollar averaging nor anything else is going to help. The only thing that the experts can accurately predict about the market, is that it will go up and it will go down. Historically, it usually finishes higher. That is why you must remember that mutual funds are for longer-term investing. Meaning, be prepared to ride out the lows while continuing to dollar average. As stated, this will bring your average price per share down, so that when the market goes up again, it only has to bring the share price above that average for you to more than break even. In other words, the market doesn't have to get all the way back to the top price for you to come out ahead. On the other hand, I know that I don't have to explain the benefits of investing in the market when it is going great.

Next, I would take full advantage whenever possible, of any tax-reducing programs you are allowed. (IRA, Keough, 401k, 403b, etc.) I would couple these tax saving plans with good mutual funds to get the best of both worlds, better returns along with tax-deferred growth. A word of caution here, and that is don't lock money into these programs if it is all that you have. These programs are for *very long term* investing, that is, money you don't intend to touch until you are at least 59 1/2. These are excellent because they let your money grow tax-deferred, but they weren't made for early withdrawals. However, there are some exceptions, so seek the advice of a qualified tax accountant or tax attorney. The difference between letting your money grow tax-deferred or not, is incredible, and could amount to hundreds of thousands of dollars, so it should not be taken lightly.

Remember, these are *tax-deferred* plans, they are not tax-free, which means that tax will be due upon distribution. However, you will hopefully be in a lower tax bracket at retirement than you are now, and your nest egg should be thousands more because of this type of plan, so it's a much better alternative than paying tax as you go.

Again, these are just programs, so you want to couple them with the vehicle that will give you a combination of the best and safest return, taking into consideration the length of time you have for your nest egg to grow.

Many people say they don't have the time to do this research. I believe you can't afford not to. As stated earlier, if you're going to work hard to get ahead, your money has got to be working hard too, or you're wasting your time.

Following are my ten rules of financial planning. They are not in any order of importance, as I believe they are all equally important.

1.) Always seek good advice.

By this I mean deal with reputable people and get more than one opinion on your investments. People usually get more than one opinion when it comes to their health, so why should it be any different for their financial health?

2.) Don't invest without first setting your goals.

Setting goals with regard to investments are no different than setting goals in any other phase of your life. You are not going to get where you want to go financially without them.

3.) Be realistic.

Don't have false expectations about your investments. Some people invest in something and expect a return that is not really feasible.

4.) Consider all types of risk.

Obviously there are investments where you could lose your entire nest egg, and there are others where your investment may be secure but you are losing ground to inflation. Just do your homework and fully understand what you are getting into.

5.) Diversify, diversify, and diversify.

Never put all of your eggs in one basket no matter how good an investment might look.

6.) Research all investments for suitability.

Your friends may tell you they have this great investment, and it may be, but not for you. Check it out.

7.) Don't fall in love with your investments.

Many people have a tendency to hang on to their first investment longer than they should, only because it was their first. That is not smart investing. Some hang on to an investment that did well once but doesn't anymore, in hopes that it will do well again. Know when to move on.

8.) Don't fall for get rich quick schemes.

The old saying is, if it sounds too good to be true, it probably is.

9.) Start now!

The longer you wait, the more money it will take each month to reach the same goal.

10.) Lastly, get a good accountant and ask a lot of questions.

Make an effort to learn the generalities of the tax laws. There is no need to become an expert, however you should learn enough to know what to ask of others. This helps you during the year to determine the basic direction in which you should be going. Don't make the mistake of waiting to begin planning your tax strategies. Proper tax planning starts in the beginning of the year, not at tax time.

Get involved, it's *your* money!

# CHAPTER FIFTEEN

## AND NOW...

Are you asking yourself, "Where do I start?" The answer is with people. This book began with an example of motivating with positives, not the negatives and scare (fear) tactics that some of us may be accustomed to seeing. I believe eventually everything comes down to people and how we treat them.

Employ the three E's in your relationships: ethics, empathy, and enthusiasm. Personal ethics form the cornerstone of all good relationships and are important because they demonstrate to people they can believe in you, that you stand for something. I don't believe anyone can be successful over the long term without a high degree of personal ethics. This is true in both business and personal relationships. All too often someone skyrockets to success, only to fizzle out a short time later because their ethics weren't in place.

Empathy shows people you care about them. The old saying is, "If you want people to care more about you, start caring more about them." The underlying theme is the "Golden Rule" of treating people the way you want to be treated.

Enthusiasm is contagious! If you have it, share it! If you don't have it, catch it! Enthusiasm has the power to lift people and inspire them to greatness. Be a generator of enthusiasm and spread it around.

Next, be determined to be a leader, of yourself first. Resolve to take charge of your life. Lead it with actions, not words. Anyone can say anything. Leaders have the habit of doing more and talking less.

Be positive as much of the time as you can. It's not easy, especially when you don't feel positive, but try. Work at it if you have to and watch it pay off in all areas of your life.

Find things to believe in, things to get excited about. It can be in any phase of your life. If you don't like what you do for a living, maybe you should try something else. Perhaps that is not necessary. Possibly just improving other areas of your life, (eg. becoming physically fit?) would improve the way you feel about yourself, which in turn would improve the way you feel about your job.

What is the bottom line? Find a cause and get charged up about improving as many phases of your life as you can! Have patience, nothing is going to work overnight. Give whatever you try a real chance and keep believing in yourself.

Speed up the learning process by finding some-one to emulate - someone who is already successful in the areas in which you want to succeed. Be a sponge, absorb all that you can!

Be on guard for the inevitable barrage of nega-tives and the people who are passing them out. The rule is simple; if you want to be more positive, seek out more positive people. Program your life for success, expect it! It will happen!

Set and record your goals for all phases of your life. Many people only have business goals. Don't stop there, have health and vacation goals too.

Now... what about you? Is this the time for you to make a commitment to yourself? Is this another book for the shelf or did you go through it with a hi-lighter and mark things that you can use again?

In the beginning I wrote that my goal was to make this book fast and easy to read. Because if it was, you, the reader, would be more likely to apply it to your life.

Many people are looking for a quick fix or magic cure for their lives. They go to seminars, buy endless numbers of tapes and books, and wonder why nothing works for them. It's not the tapes and books that aren't working, it's them. It takes work to change. It's not easy, if it was, everyone would be doing it.

A good example of this attitude is diet pills. Taking a diet pill is easier than eating properly and exercising, so that is what many people would rather do. Most people would rather take a pill to fix everything in their lives instead of doing what it takes to succeed.

While it is true that it involves a certain amount of drive to go to seminars and read books, it's just the beginning. It takes even more effort to change your attitudes and habits, and since that is not easy to do, most won't. As I stated earlier, you can't expect things to get better, if *you* don't improve. In other words, you must make these changes within you before the things around you will begin to change.

Knowledge is power only if you do something with it. You must take consistent action and be a doer not a spectator.

I have spent a lot of time discussing negatives and the fight to stay positive. I can't overemphasize the importance of a positive attitude. You get one shot at life and without a positive attitude your gun isn't even loaded.

Most people spend their entire life wishing. When you are a kid, you wish you were older. When you're old, you wish you were younger. When it's Monday, you wish it was Friday. People are never happy with today, happy with now. Quit wishing and start goal setting. Begin making it happen!

Don't be like so many who look back in their retirement years and ask themselves, "What did I do with my life?" or "I wonder what would have happened if...?"

This book is about winning. As important as reaching all of your dreams is, what is most important is just giving it your best shot. Going for it! Looking back later in life knowing that you did your best, that you didn't quit. Being proud of yourself and your effort is what really matters. Not saying, "If I had it to do over again, I wish I would have..." We are not going to get the opportunity to do it over again. This is your *only* shot so make the most of it!

You can't put your desire on the shelf because if you really want to win at life, sooner or later you have to dig in, take a stand, and fight for what you want. You have to get to the point where you are fed up and tired of losing, and you want to win so badly that you are willing to pay the price. You have to be willing to step up to the plate and swing at whatever life throws your way. It really doesn't matter whether you hit a home run or not. What's important is that you stepped up to the plate and took your best swing.

You have to want to make a difference with your

life and make it count for something! You have to want to make something happen! Don't wait for the right time to start or you never will.

It's decision time. Do you really want to make your life a success? You are the only one who can answer that question. If the answer is yes, then begin today doing the things that it takes to succeed.

The time to start is *NOW*!

Anyone can see the way things are today. Success comes to those who can turn what could be into what will be.

I wish for you the best of luck and happiness.

THE TIME TO START IS _ _ _!